A 21-Day Soul Care Devotional

Encouraging
MAMA

A 21-Day Soul Care Devotional

Encouraging
MAMA

JASMINE LOWERY

Arabelle Publishing, LLC
Chesterfield, VA

ENCOURAGING MAMA

Encouraging Mama: A 21-Day Soul Care Devotional
Copyright © 2023 Jasmine Lowery

Arabelle Publishing, LLC
Chesterfield, Virginia
www.arabellebooks.com

Bulk discounts are available if purchased through the publisher. Write to us at PO Box 2841, Chesterfield, Virginia 23832, or connect through our website or on Instagram @arabellepublishing.

Contributors:
Interior Design: Julie Basinski
Cover Design: Samuel Rog
Author's Photos: Megan Garrison Photography

Library of Congress Control Number: 2023930470
ISBN: 979-8-9862362-4-7
Printed in the United States of America

dedication

To my Lord and Savior, Jesus Christ,
who gave me the vision, strength and joy
to write this devotional.

To my loving husband, Rashad Lowery,
for faithfully supporting me in
following my God-given dreams.

To our three beautiful children,
Rashad Jr., Isaiah Mark and Joy.
Thank you for your love, patience and
all the fun memories we have built together.

To my beautiful God-fearing mother
Kathleen Portee-Sullivan, who taught me the beauty
of having a mother who wrapped her children
in unconditional love and daily prayer.

note from the author

Hey Mama!!

I pray this devotional is a breath of fresh air for you. That this is a safe space for you to run to be with your loving Heavenly Father. Whether you read this book in the morning, mid-day or evening, come prepared to receive a Word from God! You will be uplifted and encouraged. This thing called motherhood did not just happen by chance. God knew your motherhood journey wouldn't be easy, yet He still chose you for the job. He didn't call you to do it alone. Allow His Holy Spirit to fill you up! You can always count on the Holy Spirit to be your comforter, guide, and counselor as you embrace this wild and wonderful motherhood season.

TABLE OF

contents

WEARY & WORTHY

Day 1

I'm pretty sure my eyes looked like two red cherries. I was exhausted to the point my eyes burned. Two out of three of my children were up throughout the night. I was sleep-training my daughter, and my oldest was battling seasonal spring allergies. So, by the time my alarm went off, I felt far from well-rested.

Mama was grumpy and had a headache.

The icing on the cake is that my children are early risers regardless of their sleep time. So, as I dragged myself out of bed, I could hear tiny footsteps rushing towards my door.

When would I ever get a moment to myself? I was homeschooling and running my small business from home during this season of my life. So, I had a very full day ahead of me.

At this point, I only wanted to crawl into the fetal position and cry my eyes out. I had no idea how I'd muster the strength to care for my children today.

The Holy Spirit then prompted me to pray. I told my littles that mommy needed some time with GOD and invited them to lay in my bed while I stumbled into my prayer closet.

And as tears began streaming down my face, I knew GOD would see me through my day. Coffee might help energize me, but Jesus would be why love, grace, and joy flowed out of me.

But he said to me, 'My grace is sufficient for you, for my power is made perfect in weakness.' Therefore I will boast all the more gladly of my weaknesses, so that the power of Christ may rest upon me. For the sake of Christ, then, I am content with weaknesses, insults, hardships, persecutions, and calamities. For when I am weak, then I am strong.

2 Corinthians 12:9-10

Soul Care Tips

☐ ### Schedule a "quiet time" for the entire family
Play instrumental hymns and read your Bible or favorite devotional. Allow the kids to read their favorite book or draw.

☐ ### Take a nap when your child naps
Instead of music, allow your Bible App to play in the background.

☐ ### Roll on calming essential oils
Pray for strength, joy and peace.

notes

Overwhelmed in a Sinking Boat

DAY 2

There was a tower of stinky dishes in my sink. Legos and baby dolls were scattered across the floor. My children were screaming they needed more cereal. Several alarms were going off on my phone to remind me of the time-sensitive tasks I needed to complete.

My head felt like it was going to explode. Before I could gather my thoughts, I realized I had stepped into a puddle of milk.

Ah, what next, God? It felt like if it wasn't one thing, it was another. Everything was falling apart. I wanted to ball up this day and throw it in the trash can.

This was the perfect opportunity for me to humble myself. I needed GOD to put His super on my natural situation.

How many of you can relate? Desperately needing GOD to renew your heart and mind during a trying season of mothering. Be encouraged. The Holy Spirit is always near and can restore your strength.

reflect

"I have said these things to you, that in me you may have peace. In the world you will have tribulation. But take heart; I have overcome the world."

John 16:33

"And the peace of God, which surpasses all understanding, will guard your hearts and your minds in Christ Jesus."

Philippians 4:7

"God is our refuge and strength, a very present help in trouble.

Psalm 46:1

SOUL CARE TIPS

☐ ### TURN ON UPBEAT KIDS CHRISTIAN SONGS
Invite your children to help you tidy up the house.
Sing together. Create space to be silly and have fun.

☐ ### SCHEDULE A TIME FOR YOU TO SPEND ALONE
Be intentional in using that time to connect with GOD.
Having something to look forward to during the day will help
brighten your mood!

☐ ### PRAY AND INVITE GOD TO PLACE HIS
SUPER ON YOUR NATURAL SITUATION
Turn on your favorite worship song that builds your awareness of
GOD's presence and dance with your children!

notes

GRACE FOR THE GUILTY

DAY 3

I was running behind and unsure if we would make their appointment in time. Once I arrived at the parking lot, the main goal was to quickly get my toddler and newborn out of the car and run into the building.

Immediately after I slammed my car door, I attempted to open the backdoor to get my littles out. It didn't matter how hard I grabbed the handle; it wouldn't open.

I had locked my children in the car. My keys were locked inside as well.

"Who locks their children in the car? You're such a bad mom! Do you know how cold it is outside?"

I had to release that guilt and redirect my focus on getting my littles out of the locked car.

By GOD's grace, I noticed another woman walking toward the building. I explained what had happened and asked to use her phone to call the fire department.

The fire department arrived and got my babies out of the car in no time.

I pray this would serve as a reminder that God is faithful to work out even the scariest situations. Be encouraged and remember regardless of what you are experiencing, you must invite GOD into your situation.

reflect

There is therefore now no condemnation for those who are in Christ Jesus. For the law of the Spirit of life has set you free in Christ Jesus from the law of sin and death. For God has done what the law, weakened by the flesh, could not do. By sending his own Son in the likeness of sinful flesh and for sin, he condemned sin in the flesh, in order that the righteous requirement of the law might be fulfilled in us, who walk not according to the flesh but according to the Spirit.

Romans 8:1-4

SOUL CARE TIPS

☐ ### JOURNAL
Express to GOD what is making you feel guilty. Allow The Holy Spirit to guide you through ways you can change the situation or prevent it from happening in the future.

☐ ### PRAY WITH A TRUSTED FRIEND OR LEADER
Share with them what is making you feel guilty. Persue accountability if necessary.

notes

FULLY PRESENT
AND UNPLUGGED

DAY 4

Beautiful spring flowers were blooming all around us. The sky was clear, and my children's laughter filled the air.

Our family of five had arrived at one of our happy places, a local garden/petting zoo.

There were so many precious moments I knew I needed to capture. So, I put on my photographer hat and was determined to photograph as much as possible.

As I invited the kids to "say cheese" for the tenth time, I sensed The Holy Spirit leading me to put the phone away.

That was one of the best decisions I made. I was able to join in on the fun and bask in all the beauty of enjoying our happy place.

Fight the temptation to capture everything and be intentional about being in the moment with your family. Remember, the days are long, but the years fly by.

reflect

" Look carefully then how you walk, not as unwise but as wise, making the best use of the time, because the days are evil. "

Ephesians 5:15-16

respond

SOUL CARE TIPS

UNPLUG AS A FAMILY

☐ Schedule specific times during the day or week to enjoy time together without outside distractions. Use your phone timer to remind you when to plug in and unplug.

MEMORIZE SCRIPTURE

☐ Use "unplugged" moments to read the Bible together.

notes

HORMONAL AND HUMBLE

DAY 5

Where did this frog in my throat come from? No matter how hard I tried, I couldn't express to my husband what my needs were. I felt so tiny and insignificant. What in the world was wrong with me? I had just given birth to my first child less than five days ago.

It was a joyous occasion, yet something was blocking me from "feeling like myself."

Before I knew it, I was in an argument with my husband. I had thrown his phone down, and the glass shattered on our bedroom floor.

This was so out of my character that it led me to call my OBGYN. She confirmed I had a mild case of postpartum depression.

Mama, remember there is no condemnation for those in Christ Jesus. Do not walk in shame if you are experiencing "hormonal imbalances" and not feeling like yourself. Humility will help guide you into a season of healing. Take the steps needed to be well.

reflect

"

But I say, walk by the Spirit, and you will not gratify the desires of the flesh. For the desires of the flesh are against the Spirit, and the desires of the Spirit are against the flesh, for these are opposed to each other, to keep you from doing the things you want to do. But if you are led by the Spirit, you are not under the law.

Galatians 5:16-18

"

respond

Soul Care Tips

☐ **TAKE A WALK, JOG OR RUN**
Express to GOD all your worries, fears, and anxieties.

☐ **PREPARE A HEALTHY MEAL**
Aim to use fresh veggies and avoid processed food.

☐ **SET THE ALARM TO GO TO BED EARLIER**
Plan to unplug an hour before bed to ensure you're able to completely unwind.

☐ **MEMORIZE OUR "REFLECT" VERSE**
Galatians 5:16-18

notes

Treat Your Body Like a Temple

DAY 6

It was pointless for me to entertain the thought of participating in a daily running challenge. I was still shocked that someone invited me to participate in something like this.

I had three small children! My body was way out of shape. How would I make time to jog, run, skip or hop without my kids?

Yet the more I questioned it, the more I knew GOD was calling me to take on this challenge.

I committed to jogging two to three miles per day, and it changed my life. Not only did it improve my mood, but led me to make healthier eating choices. Taking multivitamins and drinking matcha tea also became a part of my healthy-living routine.

During this time The Lord also revealed to me that taking care of my body was an act of worship unto GOD. Learning to cherish my body was ultimately drawing me closer to GOD, and allowing me to show up in the world as the best version of myself.

reflect

"Or do you not know that your body is a temple of the Holy Spirit within you, whom you have from God? You are not your own, for you were bought with a price. So glorify God in your body."

1 Corinthians 6: 19-20

SOUL CARE TIPS

☐ **PRAY**

about the ways you can better care for your temple.

☐ **CREATE A PLAN**

Decide on one or two ways you can care for your temple/body, and follow through on your plan in the next one to two weeks.

notes

Down But Not Defeated

DAY 7

My body ached, and I had chills. All I wanted to do was remain superglued to my bed.

I'm pretty sure if someone had asked me what day of the week it was, I would not have been able to tell them.

In addition to my feeling horrible, negative thoughts began to fill my mind. Thoughts told me how awful of a mom I was for not being with my children right now. Thoughts that I was rejecting and neglecting them.

But what about the dishes, loads of laundry, and other household chores waiting for me to complete them?

GOD used my husband to confirm I was right where I needed to be. My body needed rest and it would not be good if I tried to force myself to do anything other than that.

Mama, you deserve to rest. Your family will reap the benefits from your obedience to care for yourself.

reflect

"He makes me lie down in green pastures. He leads me beside still waters. He restores my soul. He leads me in paths of righteousness for his name's sake.

Psalm 23:2-3
"

respond

SOUL CARE TIPS

☐ **FIND AN AUDIO VERSION OF THE BIBLE**
Listen to your favorite book in the Bible.
(Recommendations: psalms and proverbs)

☐ **MEMORIZE ONE SCRIPTURE ABOUT HEALING**
Speak it over yourself. Invite your family to speak it over you.

notes

Life is Bigger Than Money

DAY 8

I was embarrassed, yet humble enough to thank the kindhearted person blessing me.

My debit card had declined due to insufficient funds. Yet, I had essential items I needed for my family in my cart. I frantically checked my wallet for another form of payment, and a woman behind me graciously offered to pay for my items.

As I walked back to my car, tears began to stream down my face. I knew GOD was speaking to me through this situation.

I had recently given birth to my second son, and my decision to stay home drastically changed my family's financial status. Instead of adjusting my spending habits and updating the family budget, I tried to operate as if our financial situation had not changed.

I thanked GOD for His grace yet cried out for wisdom on becoming a better steward of what GOD had blessed my family with financially.

If you're currently experiencing financial hardship or need a financial blessing, I encourage you to seek GOD and wise counsel about ways you can get to a better place financially. As believers, we are called to be good stewards of our money. Yet, we walk in humility when we need support from our community.

reflect

And my God will supply every need of yours according to his riches in glory in Christ Jesus.

Philippians 4:19

respond

Soul Care Tips

☐ **Make a list**
of major financial breakthroughs you've experienced over the past three to five years.

☐ **Seek God**
on three ways you can become a better steward of your money.

☐ **Pray**
about what resources you need to invest in to become a better steward of your money. (workshops, books, or a financial coach)

notes

A Rose Can Never
Be a Sunflower

DAY 9

What was I going to do? I desperately needed a sitter, yet no one was available. My husband and I lived hours away from our parents, so that was out of the question.

Why couldn't my life be like my other mommy friends? Many of them lived minutes away from their parents. This enabled them to have support with their kids and free sitters for date nights.

This was unfair, and I was determined to have a pity party. I just had to tell GOD how awful my life was because my parents didn't live across the street from me.

Before I knew it, I began comparing my life to those other mommies. I created a Venn diagram in my mind and highlighted why their lives were better.

After a few days of sitting in this swampy space, The Holy Spirit guided me to repentance. There was an abundance of blessings GOD had given my family. Wallowing in what we didn't have only led to jealousy in my heart.

I was determined to "count it all joy," as my mother often says.

We often are jealous of others who have what we desire. I pray that we all will learn to trust GOD as our ultimate provider and rebuke the enemy's schemes to compare our lives to others.

reflect

" You make known to me the path of life; in your presence there is fullness of joy; at your right hand are pleasures forevermore. "

Psalm 16:11

respond

Soul Care Tips

☐ **Take a nature walk**
Invite the Holy Spirit to reveal ways you compare your life to others. Use this time to repent and pray for a content heart.

☐ **Write out Five scriptures**
about contentment on index cards.

☐ **Pray for the person(s)**
you were comparing yourself to.

notes

Hot Mess to Miracle

Legos were scattered everywhere, and apple juice and deli meat were smeared on the floor. There were action figures and race cars lined up on the couch.

To put icing on the cake, I had just steamed my floors.

I felt defeated.

This was a "just breath and pray, mama" moment. So, I took a deep breath, asked GOD to renew my mind, and invited the kids to help clean up.

"Okay, kids, we have four minutes and thirty seconds to quickly clean up the living room. Are you ready? We have to march around like soldiers and get the job done!".

My kids looked up at me and yelled, "yes, mama!!"

I could hardly believe my kids were excited to clean up.

As I ran to turn on the stove timer, I felt joy rise up in my heart. This would work!

They quickly began cleaning up, and when they were done, they were so proud of themselves! I was proud, too.

It felt like a modern-day miracle! Less than thirty minutes ago, they were kicking and screaming about how they didn't want to clean up.

reflect

" Whatever you do, work heartily, as for the Lord and not for men.

Colossians 3:23

Commit to the Lord whatever you do, and he will establish your plans. "

Proverbs 16:3 NIV

Soul Care Tips

☐ **Talk with your little ones about the materialistic things**

Explain to them that everything GOD has blessed your family with GOD calls us to be good stewards of them. Cleaning up and taking care of them shows gratitude to GOD.

☐ **Turn on worship music and set a timer**

Remind your littles that as we work (cleaning, completing school work, etc.) we should do our best because it is a way we show GOD how much we love and appreciate Him.

notes

PLAN OR PLAN TO FAIL

DAY 11

It was late-thirty, and the kids were finally asleep, yet my to-do list had barely been touched all day.

What was wrong with me? Oh, I know! I'm a mom. That was my excuse, and I was going to stick to it.

As I began to cry and wallow in my frustration, The Holy Spirit met me right where I was. I was reminded that without a plan, I may be planning to fail.

Once I gathered myself together, I realized that the key would be focusing on what was most important. I had to stop overwhelming myself by writing down "all the things." Delegation was also going to be my bestie. Trying to do everything myself was not wise and would only burn me out.

I also was determined to not dread doing things that needed to get done. This helps keep my heart and mind in the right place.

Mama, if you are currently frustrated because you do not feel productive, consider what ways you can begin a better planning routine. Don't forget delegation is powerful too.

reflect

"
Commit your work to the Lord, and your plans will be established.
"

Proverbs 16:3

Soul Care Tips

☐ **TURN ON INSTRUMENTAL WORSHIP MUSIC**
Write out your to-do list.

☐ **TAKE TIME TO PRAY**
Pray over your plans and decide what to delegate, or ditch for another day. Then fully submit them to GOD.

notes

notes

Happy Marriages Matter

DAY 12

Every day my goal is to not burn dinner (or breakfast or lunch). Fortunately, this evening my husband was helping me cook. Whenever we cook dinner together, we usually turn on the music. Tonight, we decided to play salsa.

In the midst of cooking dinner together, my husband grabbed my hands and began dancing with me. In front of our kids!

I initially thought, we don't have time to dance. We need to focus. And the kids are watching!

I felt uncomfortable and awkward having the kids watch us dance.

Yet, I made a choice to be in the moment. My husband held my hand and we salsa danced (the best we could).

To my surprise, the kids loved it! After awhile they even joined us.

Our children need to see that we are in love. It's so important that we model for children what a healthy marriage looks like.

Mama, don't forget a healthy marriage is genuinely one of the best gifts we can give our children.

reflect

"Two are better than one, because they have a good reward for their toil. For if they fall, one will lift up his fellow. But woe to him who is alone when he falls and has not another to lift him up! Again, if two lie together, they keep warm, but how can one keep warm alone?"

Ecclesiastes 4:9-11

SOUL CARE TIPS

☐ **WRITE A LETTER TO GOD**
Reflect on how having children has impacted your marriage.

☐ **CREATE WAYS TO BE MORE INTENTIONAL**
Jot a list of ways to intentionally model a Christ-centered marriage for your children. Invite your spouse into this process and pray as a couple over your list.

☐ **TAKE A FAMILY WALK AND TALK**
Discuss why Christ-centered marriage is a gift and honors GOD.
Note: If your spouse is not a believer, you can focus on yourself and how you plan to model Christ in your marriage.

notes

Healthy Rhythms and Routines

"Mama, what time is it? I lost my watch and need to know the time!"

This was the third time within 15 minutes that my son asked me what time it was.

I was pretty annoyed and prayed GOD would miraculously reveal his Spider-Man watch!

As frustrating as it was to tell my child the time (what felt like every time I took a breath), I was happy to know he understood that we have a schedule we go by.

The root of his asking for the time was that he wanted to ensure he was on time. I created a daily schedule for him, and he loves making sure "we are running on time."

Children crave structure and routine. As mamas, we must create a safe, loving, fun, yet structured environment for them. This consistently allows them to feel safe!

Mamas, as many of you know, in the blink of an eye, our children can attempt to run our households. It is up to us to set boundaries with them. Creating rhythms and routines is a great way to do that.

reflect

But all things should be done decently and in order.

1 Corinthians 14:40

SOUL CARE TIPS

☐ ### PRAY

about improving your current family schedule (invite older children and your spouse into this time).

☐ ### CREATE A LIST

for the entire family. Use pictures or visuals for little ones. You can place this schedule in several places in your home. *Note: Don't forget to add time with GOD to the schedule for you and the children.*

notes

notes

MOTHERHOOD IS A GIFT

DAY 14

While decluttering in my bedroom, I found a photo of myself from my honeymoon in Jamaica. I was so young and had no clue all GOD had in store for me.

Reflecting on some of my goals during that stage of my life brought me to tears. One of my prayers was that GOD would bless my marriage with children.

Fast-forwarding five years later, GOD has blessed my family with three children.

Motherhood is in no way, shape, or form a cakewalk. It requires us to sacrifice sleep, time, energy, and much more.

The day-in and the day-out hustle and bustle of motherhood can cause us to forget that what we currently have was once something we prayed for.

Mama, while mothering, do not forget the beautiful gift of motherhood.

reflect

"Children are a heritage from the Lord, offspring a reward from him. Like arrows in the hand of a warrior are children born in one's youth. Blessed is the man whose quiver is full of them.

Psalm 127: 3-5 (NIV)

respond

SOUL CARE TIPS

☐ **WRITE A LETTER TO GOD**
Reflect on a season when you desired to have children.

☐ **WRITE A SWEET NOTE TO YOUR CHILDREN**
Tell them how grateful you are for their lives.

☐ **SET ASIDE 5-10 MINUTES TO PRAISE AND WORSHIP**
GOD for the gift of motherhood

notes

notes

Boundaries in Motherhood

DAY 15

As I tip-toed downstairs, my heart filled with joy knowing my little ones were asleep. My children are early risers, so my new game plan was to start waking up at least two hours before they did to get myself prepared for the day.

I wrapped myself up in my throw blanket and pulled out my Bible. To set the atmosphere, I even began to play some instrumental hymns.

Suddenly I heard footsteps marching down the stairs. What in the world? My boys had never woken up this early before. I was so confused and upset.

I told them to hug me and that they must lie back down in their beds. If they needed a sip of water or bathroom use, they could do that quickly.

Despite my fears of their tantrums, they both returned to bed. I'm so glad I didn't walk in fear about setting boundaries with them

Mama, remember setting boundaries with our children is vital as mothers. Teaching our children when to say "yes" and how to say "no."

reflect

Let what you say be simply 'Yes' or 'No'; anything more than this comes from evil.

Matthew 5:37

SOUL CARE TIPS

☐ **JOURNAL**
about how you're setting boundaries with your children and your-self. In what ways are you doing well, and in what areas can you improve?

☐ **TAKE A FEW MOMENTS TO THANK GOD**
for being a loving Heavenly Father who sets boundaries with us.

notes

notes

Faith-filled Friendship

DAY 16

I parked my car and hopped out so quickly that I almost forgot my ignition keys. It seemed surreal that today I would be able to unite with one of my closest friends.

She was expecting her sixth baby, so this was a sweet treat to have quality time with her. Altogether we have nine children, but today we would be kid-free!

We enjoyed a yummy lunch, laughed, and shared faith-filled conversations at the most adorable restaurant. It was so nourishing to my soul to fellowship with a sister-friend who could relate to my life stage.

Mama, you deserve healthy friendships. One key I've learned about having healthy friendships while mothering children is that there must be much love and grace at the core of your sisterhood.

If you are in a season where you do not have a close friend, seek GOD on what spaces to enter where other like-minded people are. I've met some of my dearest friends anywhere from a women's bible study, a mommy's group via social media groups, local playgrounds, workout classes, or even a conference.

For those of you who do have a close friend, I encourage you to put a date on your calendar to spend together.

reflect

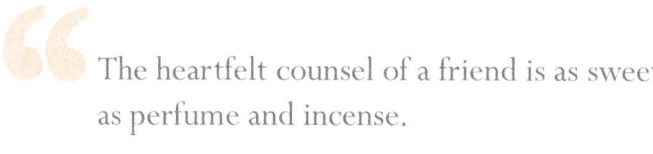
The heartfelt counsel of a friend is as sweet as perfume and incense.

Proverbs 27:9 (NLT)

SOUL CARE TIPS

☐ **INTENTIONALLY PRAY**
for your close friend and praise GOD for your sisterhood.
Note: If you are in a season where you do not have a close friend, praise GOD in advance for your friend.

☐ **HONOR YOUR FRIEND**
by providing them with a gift. Write a letter, give them a call or send them a gift showing your appreciation for their friendship.

notes

Childlike Faith

DAY 17

We repeatedly explained to our toddler son that he could not have a cell phone for Christmas.

He was adamant that he needed a phone. We tried to convince him that he could get a pretend phone, but not an actual phone. He repeatedly explained that he wanted a phone to call family and play games.

Two days before Christmas, my husband remembered he had bought an iPad for our family. This iPad could call family members and download games.

The lightbulb went off for both of us; we could add parental restrictions and give this to our son.

Our son was in awe and beyond excited that what he believed in became a reality on Christmas morning.

Mama, what things do you need to have childlike faith for? Don't get caught up with what you see in the natural realm. God is more than able to put His super on our natural situations.

reflect

"And calling to him a child, he put him in the midst of them and said, "Truly, I say to you, unless you turn and become like children, you will never enter the kingdom of heaven. Whoever humbles himself like this child is the greatest in the kingdom of heaven.

Matthew 18:2-4

SOUL CARE TIPS

☐ **JOURNAL**

about three things that require child-like faith.

☐ **LOOK UP SCRIPTURES**

about faith and choose your favorite verse. Write it on a sticky note to memorize and meditate on this week.

notes

Fill Their Love Tanks

DAY 18

"Mommy, can I come in?". This was the third day my child refused to stay downstairs with his siblings and dad while I rested.

I was so confused. Today I intentionally gave him lots of cuddles and pats on the back and cheered him on throughout the day.

Why wasn't that enough?

Instead of turning him away, I felt led to invite him to spend one-on-one time with me. We read his favorite books, and he shared all about what was going on in his world.

When it was time for dinner, he seemed like a new child. My mama's heart was so happy! While processing with my husband, we realized his love language was quality time.

I love how GOD used this moment to remind me of the importance of loving my children and how they receive love.

Mama, remember your child's love language may be different from yours (and that's okay). Be intentional in finding ways to love your child the way they want to be loved.

reflect

" And above all these put on love, which binds everything together in perfect harmony. "

Colossians 3:14

respond

SOUL CARE TIPS

☐ **TAKE THE "5 LOVE LANGUAGES" TEST**
Journal your results.

☐ **GIVE YOUR CHILDREN THE "5 LOVE LANGUAGES TEST FOR CHILDREN."**
After learning their love language, create a list of ways you can fill your child's love tank daily.

notes

Fearfully and Wonderfully Made

DAY 19

She picked up her pink rain boots, sat on the floor, and began to place her feet into each shoe. I was in awe at what I was witnessing.

My first instinct was to stop her. She was too little to do this by herself. I had never heard of a one-year-old putting on their own shoes.

The boys had never put their own shoes on this early.

The Lord began to remind me each of my children was designed uniquely. Comparing their developmental milestones, personalities, strengths, and weaknesses would only drive me insane.

So instead of trying to force my daughter into a box and make her like her brothers, I embraced this moment. I celebrated with her and even took out my phone to record a clip of her doing this.

Mama, I hope that you never take for granted that your precious child was fearfully and wonderfully made by GOD. Embrace, enjoy and rejoice in who GOD created them to be.

reflect

" I praise you, for I am fearfully and wonderfully made. Wonderful are your works; my soul knows it very well.

Psalm 139:14 "

respond

Soul Care Tips

☐ **Set aside time to look at photos of your children.**
Thank GOD for how He uniquely created each of them.

☐ **Create a list of what you're discerning**
about their gifts and talents.

☐ **Reflect on how God has uniquely created you.**
Write out a list of your gifts and talents and pray about how you use them in this life season.

notes

COMFORT IN CHRIST

DAY 20

As his head hung low, tears flowing from his eyes, he ran towards me and planted his little face into my stomach.

"Mommy, is the lightning going to hurt us?" my son anxiously asked.

I tried to comfort my son by telling him we were safe by turning the lights off and sitting quietly. At this point, I was exhausted and began worrying my son would be forever afraid of rain and lightning.

As I began to pray, my son requested to call his grandmother.

As my son poured out his fears to his grandmother, she replied that when it rains, that is a part of "GOD doing His work."

My mother comforted my son by reminding him that there are things GOD must do to properly care for His creation. This instantly relaxed my son and allowed him to rest.

Mama, remember one of the best ways we can comfort our children is through GOD's word and His promises. Teach your children about the power of spiritual warfare through prayer, scripture memorization, and worship music.

"
Blessed be the God and Father of our Lord Jesus Christ, the Father of mercies and God of all comfort, who comforts us in all our affliction, so that we may be able to comfort those who are in any affliction, with the comfort with which we ourselves are comforted by God.

2 Corinthians 1:3-4
"

respond

Soul Care Tips

☐ **Memorize a scripture**
Recite this with your children whenever they begin to worry. You can also use this same scripture when you're tempted to worry or have anxiety.

☐ **Create a playlist**
Turn it on when your child(ren) or you need to be comforted.

☐ **Have a jar where you can write out your concerns/worries.**
Pray about it and drop it in the jar!

notes

SPIRITUAL CAR WASH

DAY 21

I put my car in neutral and quickly glanced at my children sitting in the back of our minivan. Lord, I pray no one is afraid of the carwash today.

In the past, each one of my children has been afraid of the carwash. I've tried my best to explain that if we want our van to stay clean, we must take it to the car wash.

The machines used to clean the van may seem scary, but they help remove dirt we come in contact with while driving on the road.

Another aspect of taking the van to the car wash was vacuuming out the van. This helped reveal so much. There were nuggets, toys, and other miscellaneous items that popped up.

GOD reminded me of the importance of taking my soul to the Spiritual Car Wash.

I, too, can experience anxiety about allowing GOD to "clean the inside and outside" of my life. It's so much easier to keep moving forward the way I am.

The beautiful part is that regardless of how we feel as we go through the process of becoming "clean," we all can agree it's much better to drive a vehicle that has been cleaned from the inside and out.

"...he saved us, not because of works done by us in righteousness, but according to his own mercy, by the washing of regeneration and renewal of the Holy Spirit,"

Titus 3:5

respond

SOUL CARE TIPS

☐ **JOURNAL**
What are the areas you need GOD to give you a clean heart.

☐ **PLAY WORSHIP MUSIC**
about GOD giving you a "clean heart."

☐ **TALK TO YOUR CHILDREN**
about the importance of GOD giving us a pure heart.

☐ **HELP YOUR CHILDREN MAKE A LIST**
of three ways GOD can give them a clean heart.

notes

about the author

Jasmine Lowery is a wife, mommy of three, entrepreneur, speaker, Certified Christian Life Coach, an educator and author who loves encouraging women to unapologetically follow their God-given dreams. Her faith in Jesus Christ is the anchor of all she does in life.

www.ingramcontent.com/pod-product-compliance
Lightning Source LLC
Chambersburg PA
CBHW070719130626
46553CB00005B/2058